At Home
on the Ranch

Mi casa
en el rancho

Sharon Gordon

Marshall Cavendish
Benchmark
New York

I live on a ranch.

We have a lot of land.

❖

Vivo en un rancho.

Tenemos mucha tierra.

2

Our ranch has a lot of cattle.

They eat grass in big, open fields.

———————◆———————

Nuestro rancho tiene mucho ganado.

Come hierba en campos grandes y abiertos.

The cattle stay in a *corral*.

There is a fence around it.

❖

El ganado permanece en un *corral*.

Tiene una cerca alrededor.

Cowboys and cowgirls
work on the ranch.

They get up before the
sun rises.

❖

En el rancho trabajan
vaqueros y vaqueras.

Ellos se levantan antes
de que salga el sol.

They wear heavy pants and boots.

They also wear hats to block the sun.

❖

Ellos se ponen pantalones de tela gruesa y botas.

También se ponen sombreros para protegerse del sol.

The cowboys and cowgirls move the cattle to fields.

This is called a *roundup*.

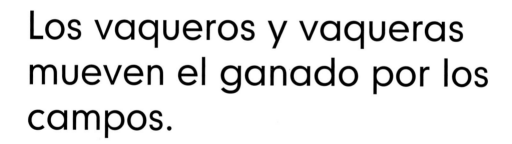

Los vaqueros y vaqueras mueven el ganado por los campos.

Esto se llama *arreo*.

The horses are a big help.

So is this helicopter!

Los caballos son una gran ayuda.

¡También lo es este helicóptero!

Sometimes the fields are far away.

It can take days to bring the cattle home.

---❖---

Algunas veces los campos están lejos.

Traer el ganado a casa puede llevar días.

The *veterinarian* comes to check our animals.

We keep notes about them on our computer.

❖

El *veterinario* viene a examinar nuestros animales.

Nosotros guardamos sus datos en nuestra computadora.

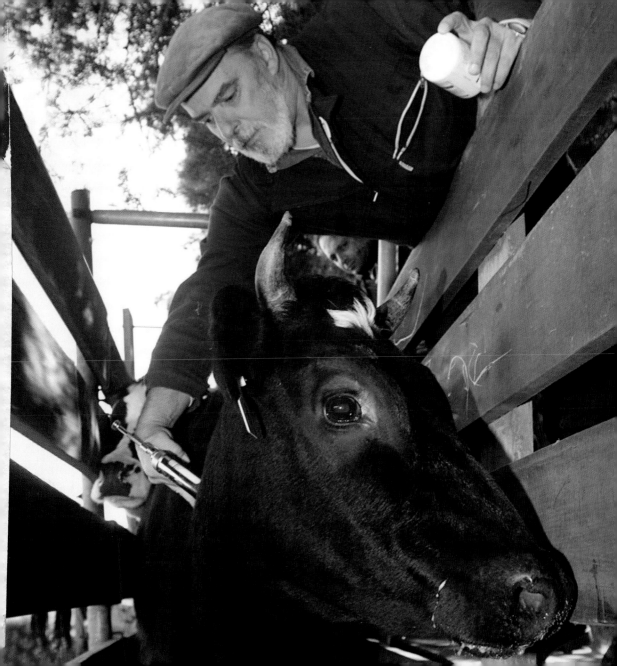

At night, we play games and tell stories.

We sing songs around the campfire.

❖

Por la noche, jugamos y contamos historias.

Cantamos canciones alrededor de la hoguera.

Some days we go to the *rodeo*.

The best riders win prizes.

———————❖———————

Vamos al *rodeo* a veces.

Los mejores jinetes ganan premios.

I am learning to ride a horse, too.

But I still need some help!

❖

Yo también estoy aprendiendo a montar a caballo.

¡Pero aún necesito ayuda!

Desert Home

La casa del rancho

cattle
ganado

corral
corral

cowgirl
vaquera

rodeo
rodeo

roundup
arreo

veterinarian
veterinario

Challenge Words

corral A fenced in place for holding horses or cattle.

rodeo A contest in which cowboys and cowgirls test their skills.

roundup To gather together cattle and move them from place to place.

veterinarian A doctor who cares for animals.

Palabras avanzadas

arreo Reunir el ganado y moverlo de un lugar a otro.

corral Un lugar con una cerca para contener los caballos o el ganado.

rodeo Una competencia en la que los vaqueros y vaqueras prueban su habilidad.

veterinario Un doctor que atiende a los animales.

29

Index

Page numbers in **boldface** are illustrations.

Índice

Las páginas indicadas con números en **negrita** tienen ilustraciones.

About the Author
Datos biográficos de la autora

Sharon Gordon has written many books for young children. She has always worked as an editor. Sharon and her husband Bruce have three children, Douglas, Katie, and Laura, and one spoiled pooch, Samantha. They live in Midland Park, New Jersey.

Sharon Gordon ha escrito muchos libros para niños. Siempre ha trabajado como editora. Sharon y su esposo Bruce tienen tres niños, Douglas, Katie y Laura, y una perra consentida, Samantha. Viven en Midland Park, Nueva Jersey.

31

With thanks to Nanci Vargus, Ed.D. and
Beth Walker Gambro, reading consultants

Marshall Cavendish Benchmark
99 White Plains Road
Tarrytown, New York 10591-9001
www.marshallcavendish.us

Library of Congress Cataloging-in-Publication Data

Gordon, Sharon.
[At home on the ranch Spanish & English]
At home on the ranch = Mi casa en el rancho / Sharon Gordon. — Bilingual ed.
p. cm. — (Bookworms. At home = Mi casa)
Includes index.
ISBN-13: 978-0-7614-2458-1 (bilingual edition)
ISBN-10: 0-7614-2458-X (bilingual edition)
ISBN-13: 978-0-7614-2378-2 (Spanish edition)
ISBN-10: 0-7614-1962-4 (English edition)
1. Ranching—Juvenile literature. 2. Ranch life—Juvenile literature. I. Title. II. Title:
Mi casa en el rancho. III. Series: Gordon, Sharon. Bookworms. At home (Spanish & English)

SF197.5.G6718 2006b
636'.01—dc22
2006016721

Spanish Translation and Text Composition by Victory Productions, Inc.
www.victoryprd.com

Photo Research by Anne Burns Images

Cover Photo by Corbis/David Stoecklein

The photographs in this book are used with permission and through the courtesy of:
Corbis: pp. 1, 17 Richard T. Nowitz; p. 3 Mark E. Gibson; pp. 5, 28 (upper l.) Darrell Gulin;
p. 9 David Stoecklein; p. 19 Bob Rowan; pp. 21, 29 (right) Reuters; p. 23 Mark Peterson;
pp. 25, 28 (lower r.) Paul A. Souders; p. 27 Jan Butchofsky-Houser.
Index Stock Imagery: pp. 7, 28 (upper r.) Peggy Koyle; pp. 11, 28 (lower l.) Robert Dawson.
Peter Arnold: pp. 13, 29 (left) Joel Bennett; pp. 15 Bilderberg/Ginter.

Series design by Becky Terhune

Printed in Malaysia
1 3 5 6 4 2